THE INVENTION OF THE
ASSEMBLY LINE

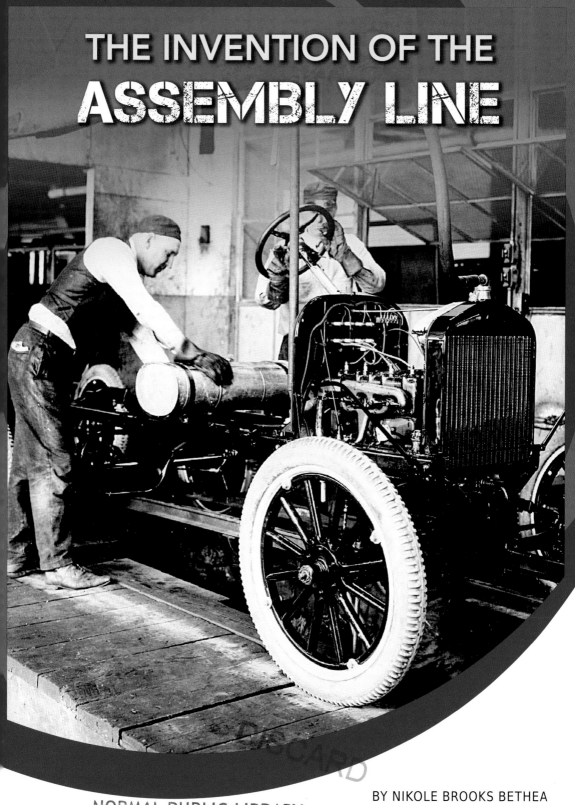

BY NIKOLE BROOKS BETHEA

Published by The Child's World®
1980 Lookout Drive • Mankato, MN 56003-1705
800-599-READ • www.childsworld.com

Photographs ©: Detroit Publishing Co./Library of Congress, cover, 1, 8; Chicago
Architectural Photographing Company/Library of Congress, 6; Hartsook/Library of
Congress, 9; Library of Congress, 10, 12, 13, 14; Everett Collection/Newscom, 16;
Bettmann/Getty Images, 17; National Motor Museum Heritage Images/Newscom,
18, 22, 24; Red Line Editorial, 20; Marion Post Wolcott/Library of Congress, 25; Ann
Rosener/Library of Congress, 26; Rainer Plendl/Shutterstock Images, 28

ISBN 9781503816367
LCCN 2016945627

Printed in the United States of America
PA02321

ABOUT THE AUTHOR
Nikole Brooks Bethea is a licensed professional engineer. She earned a
bachelor's and master's degree in environmental engineering from the
University of Florida and worked as a professional engineer for 15 years.
Most of Mrs. Bethea's publications are science and engineering books
for children.

TABLE OF
CONTENTS

FAST FACTS

- The first assembly line was developed in 1913. It happened at the Highland Park Ford Plant near Detroit, Michigan.

- Before the assembly line, it took more than 12 hours to build a Model T. After the assembly line, it took only 93 minutes.

- The Model T had 3,000 parts. The assembly line process broke down production into 84 different steps.

- Ford's assembly line eventually produced a Model T every 24 seconds. By 1927, more than 15 million of the cars had been sold. This made up half of the cars sold at the time.

- Henry Ford did not invent the assembly line. It evolved from trial and error. Ford hired talented managers who experimented. Some key people were Clarence Avery, Charles Sorensen, and P. E. Martin. Others included Carl Emde, William Klann, and William Knudsen.

TIMELINE

June 1903: The Ford Motor Company is formed.

1906: Henry Ford becomes president of Ford Motor Company.

October 1, 1908: The Model T Ford is shown for the first time.

January 1, 1910: The Highland Park Ford Plant opens.

April 1, 1913: An assembly line making flywheel **magnetos** begins operating. The flywheel magnetos are part of the Model T's electrical system.

August 1913: A Model T chassis assembly line begins operating.

1914: Ford doubles assembly line workers' **wages** to $5 per day.

1924: Ford produces the 10 millionth Model T.

1927: Ford produces the 15 millionth Model T.

May 26, 1927: Production of the Model T stops.

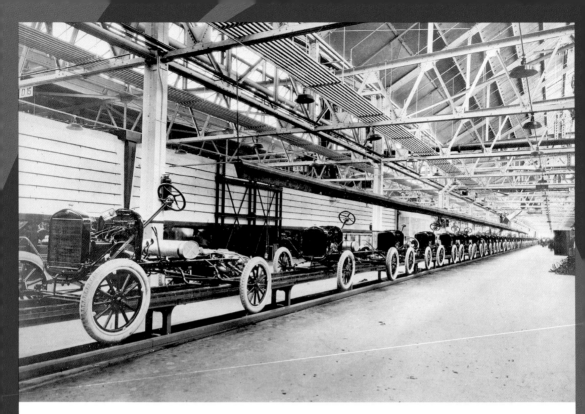

Chapter 1

A BIG RAISE

Five dollars a day! The worker couldn't believe it. His boss, Henry Ford, had more than doubled his wage. The newspaper headline read, "Henry Ford Gives $10,000 in 1914 Profits to His Employees."[1] The worker was an employee at the Highland Park Ford Plant near Detroit, Michigan. He built Model T cars every day. He had earned less than $2.50 a day when he started working there four years earlier in 1910.

The Model T cost $780 then. It would have taken 312 days' worth of wages to buy one. That was far more than the worker could afford.

The Highland Park Ford Plant had opened in 1910. The factory was very modern. Mr. Ford had installed electrical power and lights all through the factory. That meant workers could still make cars when it was dark outside.

The most modern part of the factory was the assembly line. The Model T had been introduced in 1908. Back then, teams of workers built entire cars. Now, with the assembly line, the work was divided into parts. Teams of workers did not build entire cars anymore. Instead, workers did the same job over and over. Their work moved to them on **conveyors** and gravity slides. The conveyors moved the parts from worker to worker. Gravity slides allowed parts to be sent from higher to lower levels in the factory.

Mr. Ford wanted the Model T to be a car the average American could afford. Using the assembly line, Mr. Ford could produce cars more quickly. That meant he had more cars to sell. He could also make them cheaper. By 1914, the price of the Model T had dropped to $490. And the worker's wage had been doubled. Now the Model T cost only 98 days' worth of wages.

▲ **When the Highland Park Ford Plant opened, it was one of the largest facilities in the world.**

At last, the worker could afford the Model T he had always dreamed of owning!

The worker's new wage was great. But now his job was very boring. Before the assembly line existed, Mr. Ford employed teams of skilled workers. These workers were not fast, though. The goal of the assembly line was speed. Mr. Ford needed **mass production** to meet customers' demand for the Model T. He broke down the work into small, **repetitive** tasks. Unskilled workers did these jobs.

The worker felt his job was mindless. He tightened the same screws all day. The cars rolled past him one after another. They were all exactly the same. Mr. Ford joked, "Any customer can have a car painted any color that he wants so long as it is black."[2]

The work may have been dull, but the assembly line was **efficient**. Back in 1910, the company had produced only 20,727 Model T cars. Now, in 1914, the company produced 230,788.

▲ **Henry Ford became one of the richest people in the world after the assembly line helped his company achieve success.**

Chapter 2

BORROWING THE BEST IDEAS

Henry Ford first saw a gasoline-powered horseless carriage at the 1893 World's Fair. Since then, he had been obsessed with building automobiles. He began the Ford Motor Company in 1903. It was his third attempt at an automobile company. He knew he had to do things differently if this company was going to be successful.

In 1906, Ford was interviewed for a magazine called *Automobile*. "The greatest need today is a light, low-priced car," he said. "It must be powerful enough for American roads and capable of carrying its passengers anywhere that a horse-drawn vehicle will go."[3]

In 1908, Ford worked with his best mechanics. They built the first Model T. Soon, Ford received orders for 15,000 cars. To assemble the Model T, teams of workers moved from station to station performing tasks. Ford timed his workers. It took more than 12 hours to build a Model T in this way. That was too slow, Ford thought.

Ford remembered visiting the mail-order processing plant of Sears, Roebuck and Company. It had opened in 1906 in Chicago, Illinois. Ford had toured the plant in amazement. Everywhere he looked, he saw time-saving technology. He watched as items moved along conveyors. He saw packages fall through gravity chutes. In other parts of the warehouse, he saw elevators, moving sidewalks, and endless chains operating. He watched as pneumatic tubes used air to move packages. Ford was inspired. These technologies worked together to improve productivity.

Ford also learned about modern technologies used in other industries. He made another trip to Chicago with his engineers.

▲ **Chicago meatpacking plants used conveyors to move meat around the building.**

Some of the most modern factories in the United States were there. Ford and his engineers toured several meatpacking plants. Live animals entered the building. The products were meat, hides, and animal fat. Ford watched the overhead trolleys moving beef and pork from worker to worker. He noted how this sped up meat production. The work came to the worker. The worker did not move to the work.

Chicago's canning industry also offered insight to Ford. Here, cans were being mass-produced to be used for the food industry.

The machines were arranged in the order in which they were used in the process. Conveyors connected the machines. This allowed continuous flow of work to the workers.

Henry Ford returned to Detroit. He was impressed with the processes he had seen used in other industries. He thought about these time-saving methods. Then he began making plans for improving his own productivity.

▲ **The canning industry used moving belts so that workers could stay in one place.**

Chapter 3

ASSEMBLY LINE EXPERIMENTS

A factory worker stood at his workspace at the Highland Park Ford Plant. He was amazed at the talented engineers and managers he worked under. Together, Mr. Ford's team knew about all the best **manufacturing** technologies used in the United States. There were machinists who had worked in flour mills and breweries.

◀ By 1913, Ford was producing more than 100,000 Model T cars per year.

They were familiar with grain elevators and conveyors. There were experts from the sewing-machine industry. Others were familiar with the canning and food-processing industry. Mr. Ford drew on his team's different areas of expertise. The team constantly experimented to improve production.

On April 1, 1913, the factory worker found that his workspace had changed. Normally, he stood at a workbench. His job was to assemble an entire flywheel magneto. This was the main part of the electrical generating system for the Model T. Day after day, the worker had placed 16 magnets and 16 bolts, plus the clamps and supports, into each flywheel magneto.

But today, he found no individual workbenches. Instead, he found a long row of flywheels. The flywheels lay on top of a smooth, waist-high surface. The instructions from the boss seemed odd. He told the workers they would not be building a flywheel magneto. Instead, they would be placing one part into each flywheel magneto. Then, each worker would slide the flywheel magneto along the surface to the next worker. This process was repeated over and over for the entire workday.

It didn't take the worker long to realize that not everyone worked at his same speed. He placed his part into the flywheel.

▲ **Workers assemble flywheel magnetos in the Ford plant.**

Then he slid it down the line. But he was soon stacking them in a growing pile. The person who received his parts worked slower than he did. Sometimes, he had to wait for the previous worker to pass a flywheel to him.

The managers eventually evened out the working speed. They moved the flywheels with a continuous chain. Now the flywheels all moved at the same rate. That meant all the workers had to work at the same speed. Before this new process, each flywheel had taken the worker 15 minutes to build at his workbench. Now, each flywheel was built in only five minutes.

**The conveyor belt continues moving as workers ▶
assemble generators.**

Chapter 4

PUTTING AN ASSEMBLY LINE IN OPERATION

In August 1913, another experiment was happening at the Highland Park Ford Plant. The worker heard managers talking about the chassis assembly process. The chassis was the car's frame. The managers hoped for the same success as with the flywheel magneto.

The worker saw that people had attached a rope to the chassis. The rope was attached to a **windlass**. It towed the chassis along the factory floor. Engineers had spaced parts along the pathway.

The worker watched a small team of assemblers follow the chassis. The team installed the parts as they came to them. The managers were thrilled to see that this experiment cut assembly time of the chassis in half. Assembly was reduced from more than 12 hours to only 6 hours.

The worker thought about how this new assembly process was different from the way he had been building cars before. Workers had laid out the front and rear **axles**. Then the chassis frame was connected to the axles. Next, the wheels were added to the axles. More parts were added until the car was built in place. All those parts had to be carried by hand to each assembling station. If there were 100 assembling stations, 500 assemblers were needed. Another 100 workers were required to carry parts to the assembling stations.

As the days passed, the worker saw the assembly line experiments continue. The chassis assembly process improved. On October 7, he counted 140 assemblers spaced along a 150-foot (46-m) assembly line.

The workers completed 435 chassis in a single workday. The assembly of each chassis took 2 hours and 57 minutes. The assembly line was cutting down on production time.

MODEL T PRODUCTION

YEAR	PRICE OF CAR	NUMBER OF CARS PRODUCED	NUMBER OF CARS SOLD
1909	$950	13,840	12,292
1910	$780	20,727	19,293
1911	$690	53,488	40,402
1912	$600	82,388	78,611
1913	$550	189,088	182,809
1914	$490	230,788	260,720
1915	$440	394,788	355,276
1916	$360	585,388	577,036

By December 1913, he noticed that the chassis assembly line had grown to 300 feet (91 m) long. This gave the 177 men spaced along the line more room to work. The workers completed 606 chassis in a workday. The production time was reduced to 2 hours and 38 minutes. The experiments were working. Production was getting faster!

The experiments continued. By the end of December, the worker saw two assembly lines. There were 191 workers stationed along the lines. The cars were pushed manually along the line. The workers were able to complete 642 chassis in a workday. But the production time had increased to 2 hours and 42 minutes. This experiment was not successful. Something new had to be tried.

In early 1914, the engineers installed a chain to pull the cars along. By April of that year, three assembly lines were operating. Chassis assembly time was reduced to 1 hour and 33 minutes. The worker could hardly believe it. Less than a year ago, the assembly time had been 12 hours.

The worker glanced around the factory. He noticed how much the factory had changed since he began working there. There were mazes of conveyors, powered drive belts, and gravity slides everywhere he looked.

Chapter 5

IMPROVING THE DESIGN

The worker was happy when the Ford plant started using **interchangeable** parts. Before interchangeable parts were produced, assembling a car was often a hassle. Parts didn't always fit together properly. During assembly, he had to hand-fit many of the parts. This often required last-minute sanding or filing.

Bolts sometimes wouldn't fit through small holes in the parts. That meant he had to drill larger holes so bolts could be inserted.

But now, things were different. Standardized parts had greatly improved production. Every part was made to be identical. Each valve that was manufactured should fit in each engine that was built. To produce identical parts, Ford had to improve the precision of the machines that made the parts.

Installing single-purpose machines at the Ford factory made work move faster. In the past, Ford's tool experts adjusted individual machines to make many different parts. It took time to precisely adjust each setting. Mr. Ford wanted the assembly line to be efficient. Therefore, machines were set to perform only one task. That meant the worker could work much faster. He didn't have to wait for machines to be adjusted.

The worker looked at the arrangement of tools along Ford's assembly line. It was very different from any factory he had worked in before. Other factories grouped all of the same type of machinery together. For example, all punch presses were located in one area. All drilling machines were located in another. But the Ford plant placed machines along the assembly line in the order they were used. That meant the worker didn't have to run from one area to another to use equipment.

▲ **Workers stuff the seat cushions on a line of Model T cars.**

Everything was conveniently located. A punch press, drilling machine, furnace, and grinder could be found side by side along the assembly line in Ford's plant.

Mr. Ford had a Time Study Department. The worker thought it was a nuisance. Jobs were broken down into small tasks. Each of these tasks had to be completed in nearly equal time. But each time a part was changed, the Time Study Department timed the workers. And when another adjustment was made, the workers were timed again. One worker said, "they followed engineering changes very closely . . . and immediately would study the job and adjust their time study."[4]

The worker constantly felt pressured to work faster and faster. "You get toughened to the job in a matter of weeks and from then on it doesn't both you," said another worker.[5] Any problems had to be addressed quickly. Ford kept bicycles on the factory floor. When a problem came up, problem-solvers hopped onto bikes and rushed to take care of it.

But all of these time-saving procedures were working. Model T Fords were rolling off the assembly line faster and faster. Improvement in the assembly line design resulted in increases in production.

▲ **The Model T became the first car that working-class people could afford.**

Chapter 6

THE ASSEMBLY LINE'S IMPACT

The worker listened to President Roosevelt's speech on the radio. "Our nation will and must speak from every assembly line," Roosevelt said. "Our factories and our shipyards are constantly expanding. Our output must be multiplied."[6] It was October 1941, and World War II was underway.

The United States was not yet involved in the war, but it seemed like only a matter of time.

A few weeks later, Japanese planes attacked Pearl Harbor, Hawaii. The United States was now in the war. The worker thought back to the president's speech. The United States had embraced the assembly line. Mass production was considered crucial to victory.

The worker was now employed at the Ford River Rouge Complex. He worked on the assembly line making jeeps for the U.S. military. Ford Motor Company had converted two square miles of its River Rouge plant into war machine production.

Ford Motor Company wasn't the only automobile manufacturer producing tools of war. The U.S. government also had contracts with General Motors, Chrysler, Packard, Studebaker, and Hudson. The auto manufacturers' assembly lines were producing trucks, airplanes, tanks, and cannons.

Wartime demands required constant innovation. As war needs changed, the military demanded improvements in war machines. Assembly lines had to become flexible. After the war, manufacturers used these new technologies to produce consumer goods.

▲ **By the 2000s, many parts of the assembly line were operated by robots instead of people.**

The worker never dreamed that Mr. Ford's experiments almost 30 years earlier would have had such an impact on the country. But mass production of the Model T had indeed made it affordable for the average American. Owning vehicles had given people freedom to travel. They were no longer dependent on trains. Automobiles connected rural areas with the cities. People had the freedom to live where they desired. As people settled outside the cities, the suburbs grew.

Mr. Ford was proud of the success of the assembly line. His willingness to share his technology allowed it to spread quickly throughout American manufacturing. Within a decade of Ford's development of the assembly line, household items such as vacuum cleaners, radios, and phonographs were being produced on assembly lines.

Even farms became automated. In 1930, farmers began milking cows by machines rather than by hand. It was possible to milk 250 cows per hour with automated milkers. After the introduction of the assembly line, the world would never be the same again.

THINK ABOUT IT

- How was production of the automobile different before and after invention of the assembly line process?
- How would everyday life have changed for people when they were able to buy an automobile?
- What reasons might Henry Ford have had for increasing workers' wages?
- What were some of the steps Henry Ford took to make his assembly line more efficient?

GLOSSARY

axles (AX-uhlz): Axles are the rods or shafts passing through the center of wheels. The workers put the wheels on the car's axles.

conveyors (kun-VEY-urz): Conveyors are machines that enable objects to move from one place to another. The conveyors moved car parts across the factory so that workers could stay in one place.

efficient (i-FISH-unt): Efficient means producing the maximum results with the minimum wasted effort, time, or materials. Henry Ford developed an efficient assembly line process.

interchangeable (in-ter-CHAYN-juh-buhl): Interchangeable means able to be replaced with one another. Henry Ford used interchangeable parts to build the Model T.

magneto (mag-NEE-toz): Magnetos were parts that supplied energy to ignite the engines. The Model T's ignition system relied on magnetos to provide electricity.

manufacturing (man-yuh-FAK-chur-ing): Manufacturing is the process of turning raw materials into finished products, especially in a factory. Henry Ford's assembly line modernized the manufacturing process.

mass production (MASS pruh-DUK-shun): Mass production is the manufacture of standardized products in large quantities. Mass production of war machines occurred during World War II.

repetitive (re-PET-i-tiv): Repetitive means repeating again and again. Workers performed repetitive tasks on the assembly line.

wages (WAYJ-iz): Wages are the amounts that workers get paid. In 1914, Henry Ford increased daily wages to $5.00 per worker.

windlass (WIND-luhs): A windlass is a device used to haul or lift a weight or load. The windlass pulled the chassis along the factory floor.

SOURCE NOTES

1. "The Five-Dollar Day—Jump-Starting the Middle Class." *Henry Ford 150.* MotorCities National Heritage Area, n.d. Web. 20 June 2016.

2. Henry Ford and Samuel Crowther. *My Life and Work.* Garden City, NY: Doubleday, Page & Company, 1923. 72. Internet Archive. Web. 29 June 2016.

3. David A. Hounshell. *From the American System to Mass Production, 1800–1932: The Development of Manufacturing Technology in the United States.* Baltimore: Johns Hopkins University Press, 1984. Print. 218.

4. David E. Nye. *America's Assembly Line.* Cambridge, MA: MIT Press, 2013. Print. 23.

5. Ibid.

6. Ibid. 128.

TO LEARN MORE

Books

Abrams, Dennis. *The Invention of the Moving Assembly Line: A Revolution in Manufacturing.* New York: Chelsea House, 2011.

Burgan, Michael. *Who Was Henry Ford?* New York: Grosset & Dunlap, 2014.

Royston, Angela. *Henry Ford and the Assembly Line.* New York: PowerKids Press, 2016.

Web Sites

Visit our Web site for links about the invention of the assembly line:

childsworld.com/links

Note to Parents, Teachers, and Librarians: We routinely verify our Web links to make sure they are safe and active sites. So encourage your readers to check them out!

INDEX